I Like Biographies!

Read About
Walt Disney

Stephen Feinstein

© Disney Enterprises, Inc.

Enslow Elementary

an imprint of

Enslow Publishers, Inc.

40 Industrial Road   PO Box 38
Box 398   Aldershot
Berkeley Heights, NJ 07922   Hants GU12 6BP
USA   UK

http://www.enslow.com

Words to Know

animation—A moving picture cartoon.

animator—A person who makes moving picture cartoons.

cartoonist—Someone who draws cartoons.

theme park—A park for families with many rides and attractions.

Enslow Elementary, an imprint of Enslow Publishers, Inc.

Enslow Elementary® is a registered trademark of Enslow Publishers, Inc.

Library of Congress Cataloging-in-Publication Data

Feinstein, Stephen.
   Read about Walt Disney / Stephen Feinstein.—1st ed.
      p. cm. — (I like biographies!)
   Includes bibliographical references and index.
   ISBN 0-7660-2595-0
   1. Disney, Walt, 1901–1966—Juvenile literature.
2. Animators—United States—Biography—Juvenile literature. I. Title. II. Series.
   NC1766.U52D53295 2005
   741.5'8'092—dc22
                2004026782

Printed in the United States of America

10 9 8 7 6 5 4 3 2 1

Contents

© Disney Enterprises, Inc.

Walt Disney was born in Chicago on December 5, 1901. When Walt was five, his family moved to a farm in Missouri. Everyone except for Ruth, the baby girl, had jobs to do. Walt's mother, Flora, sold food she cooked and butter she made. Walt's three older brothers worked in the fields with their father, Elias. Walt took care of the pigs, chickens, and ducks.

Walt Disney grew up to be one of the world's most famous cartoonists.

Walt was happy on the farm. He played in the fields with his sister. He loved the farm animals and gave them names. Walt liked to draw pictures of the animals.

This is Walt and his little sister, Ruth. They loved to play on their farm.

7

In 1910, the family sold the farm and moved to Kansas City, Missouri. Walt and his brother Roy worked for their father. They delivered newspapers. The boys began working at 3:30 A.M. Walt was always tired, but he still found time to draw. He took drawing lessons at the Art Institute.

Here are Walt's parents, Flora and Elias Disney.

9

When Walt was fifteen, the family moved back to Chicago. Walt studied art and cartooning. Then he got a movie camera. He learned how to make animated cartoons.

Walt told his father he was going to be an artist. But Elias told Walt that he would never be able to make a living that way. Still, Walt's mind was made up.

This is one of Walt's cartoons. It shows Donald Duck and his nephews.

Walt went to Kansas City in the fall of 1919. There he got a job drawing cartoons for ads. But Walt's dream was to make animated cartoons. So Walt and his friend Ub Iwerks went into business together. They made seven cartoons, but they could not make money.

In this picture, Walt (on the right) is working with two animators to make a cartoon.

In July 1923, Walt joined his brother Roy in California. Neither of them could find a job, so they started the Disney Brothers Studio. It was the first animated cartoon studio in Hollywood. In 1924, Ub Iwerks joined the Disney brothers and became the studio's top animator.

In 1925, Walt married Lillian Bounds. Later they had two daughters, Diane and Sharon.

The Disney Brothers Studio made short cartoons, but business was slow. Walt was worried. He knew that the studio had to make more money.

One day, Walt was riding a train from New York to Hollywood. He looked at the drawing pad on his lap. Suddenly, an idea popped into his mind! Walt began drawing a cute little mouse. He called the mouse Mickey.

Walt called his cartoon mouse Mickey. The little mouse made people laugh, and everyone loved him.

© Disney Enterprises, Inc.

17

On November 18, 1928, Walt Disney's *Steamboat Willie* opened in New York. It starred Mickey Mouse. *Steamboat Willie* was the world's first cartoon with sound. The film was soon playing all across the country.

The Disney Studio grew bigger and bigger. Walt hired hundreds of artists. He showed them how to be animators.

Some of Walt's movies used real animals, too. Here he is trying to get a penguin to perform for the camera.

In 1937, Walt's *Snow White and the Seven Dwarfs*, the first full-length cartoon, was a huge hit. *Cinderella, Pinocchio, Bambi,* and many other movies were big hits, too. In 1955, Walt opened the world's first theme park, Disneyland.

Walt Disney died on December 15, 1966, after bringing joy to people all over the world.

Here is Walt at Disneyland Park with his grandson. Today The Walt Disney Company includes movie studios, a TV network, and theme parks in California, Florida, France, and Japan.

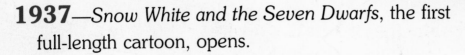

Timeline

1901—Walt Disney is born in Chicago, Illinois, on December 5.

1906—Walt's family moves to a farm in Missouri.

1920—Walt and Ub Iwerks form a company to make animated films.

1923—Walt moves to Hollywood, California. He and his brother Roy form the Disney Brothers Studio.

1925—Walt Disney and Lillian Bounds get married.

1928—Walt creates Mickey Mouse. Mickey stars in *Steamboat Willie*, the first sound cartoon.

© Disney Enterprises, Inc.

1937—*Snow White and the Seven Dwarfs*, the first full-length cartoon, opens.

1955—Disneyland Park opens.

1966—Walt Disney dies on December 15.

Learn More

Books

Hammontree, Marie. *Walt Disney: Young Movie Maker.* New York: Aladdin Paperbacks, 1997.

Jardine, Don. *Creating Cartoon Animals.* Laguna Hills, Calif.: Walter Foster Publishing, 1997.

Parent, Nancy, editor. *Disney's Storybook Collection.* New York: Disney Press, 1998.

Preszler, June. *Walt Disney: A Photo-Illustrated Biography.* Mankato, Minn.: Bridgestone Books, 2004.

Web Sites

Disney Characters
<http://disney.go.com>

Click on "Visit the Neighborhoods," then click on "Character Gallery."

The Walt Disney Family Museum: Children's Guide
<http://disney.go.com>

Click on "Inside Disney," then click on "Family Museum," then click on "Children's Guide to Walt."

Index